SEBASTIAN DUNN

GROUP PSYCHOLOGY AND THE ANALYSIS OF THE EGO

Exploring the Dynamics of
Group Behavior and Individual Identity
(2024 Guide for Beginners)

Copyright © 2024 by Sebastian Dunn

All rights reserved. No part of this publication may be reproduced, stored or transmitted in any form or by any means, electronic, mechanical, photocopying, recording, scanning, or otherwise without written permission from the publisher. It is illegal to copy this book, post it to a website, or distribute it by any other means without permission.

First edition

This book was professionally typeset on Reedsy. Find out more at reedsy.com

Contents

1. I. Introduction — 1
2. II. Le Bon's Description of the Group Mind — 3
3. Other Accounts of Collective Mental Life — 10
4. IV. Suggestion and Libido — 14
5. V. Two Artificial Groups: The Church and the Army — 19
6. VI. Further Problems and Lines of Work — 23
7. VII. Identification — 27
8. VIII. Being in Love and Hypnosis — 31
9. IX. The Herd Instinct — 36
10. X. The Group and the Primal Horde — 40
11. A Differentiating Grade in the Ego — 45
12. XII. Postscript — 49

1

I. Introduction

When the differences between Individual Psychology and Social or Group1 Psychology are compared more carefully, the initially stark differences between them become less so. It is true that individual psychology focuses on the individual and investigates the means by which he tries to satiate his instincts; however, individual psychology is rarely — and only in very specific circumstances — able to ignore the relationships that this individual has with others. Someone else is always engaged in the person's mental existence, either as an opponent, a helper, an object, a model, or both. For this reason, from the beginning, individual psychology is also social psychology.

In the previously mentioned relationships, the person is influenced by one or a very small group of individuals who have all grown to be very important to him. These individuals include his parents, brothers, sisters, the person he is in love with, his friend, and his doctor. Now, when discussing social or group psychology, it has become customary to ignore these relationships and focus instead on the influence of many people on one person at once — people he is connected to in some way, even though they may otherwise be complete strangers to him.

Group psychology is still in its infancy, but even so, it encompasses a vast array of distinct challenges and presents researchers with innumerable problems that were previously improperly differentiated from one another. The simple act of classifying the various group formation processes and describing the mental events they give birth to demands a significant amount of observation and explanation, and has already created a wealth of literature. It should be obvious to anybody comparing the scope of Group Psychology with the constrained parameters of this little book that just a select handful of the topics covered in it will be covered here. Furthermore, there will only be a few number of questions that the psychoanalysis's depth psychology will address.

2

II. Le Bon's Description of the Group Mind

Le Bon: Group Mind

- Le Bon's idea that **crowds foster anonymity** and sometimes generate emotion has become somewhat of a cliché. Yet, it has been contested by some critics, such as Clark McPhail who points out that some studies show that "the **madding crowd**" does not take on a life of its own, apart from the thoughts and intentions of members.

It would seem more beneficial to begin with an indication of the scope of the phenomena under consideration rather than with a definition, and then to pick a few particularly noteworthy and distinctive facts from among them to which our investigation may be tied. By using a statement from Le Bon's justifiably well-known book Psychologie des foules, we may accomplish both of these goals.

Let's clarify everything one more. If psychology, which studies a person's inclinations, instincts, motivations, and goals down to his actions and relationships with those closest to him, had finished its work and resolved all of these issues and their connections, it would then.

To respond to these three inquiries is the responsibility of a theoretical group psychologist. It seems obvious that starting with the third is the best way to tackle them. The information for group psychology is derived from observations of the individual's changing reactions, as every attempt at explanation necessitates a description of the object of explanation.

I'll now give Le Bon the benefit of the doubt. "The most notable peculiarity presented by a psychological group3 is the following," he states. Regardless of the individuals that make up this group, whether they are similar or unlike in their lifestyle, careers, personalities, or intelligence, the fact that they have united as a unit gives them.

We'll feel free to add a gloss of our own to Le Bon's explanation, and as a result, we'll insert a comment here.

If the members of the group are brought together to form a unity, then there must be a common link between them, and this tie may be what makes a group unique. However, Le Bon does not address this issue; instead, he discusses the changes that people go through when they are in a group and does it in a way that is consistent with the core ideas of our own depth psychology.

II. LE BON'S DESCRIPTION OF THE GROUP MIND

Le Bon believes that when people join a group, their unique qualities are erased, and as a result, they lose their individuality.

The diverse becomes enmeshed in the homogenous, giving rise to the racial unconscious. We may argue that the unconscious foundations, which are universal in all people, are revealed to view, and that the mental superstructure, whose growth in individuals displays such differences, is eliminated.

Individuals within a group would eventually exhibit ordinary character in this way. However, Le Bon feels that they also exhibit novel traits that they did not have before, and he looks for three distinct causes for this.

The first is that a person who joins a group only gains a membership due to numerical factors.

From our perspective, we don't need to give the appearance of new traits a lot of weight. For us, it would enough to remark that inside a group, the person is placed in circumstances that enable him to resist the urges of his unconscious mind. Then, he exhibits seemingly fresh traits that are actually expressions of this unconscious, which is the reservoir of all that is negative and predisposed in the human mind. Under such circumstances, it is easy for us to see why conscience and responsibility have vanished. We have long maintained that the fundamental component of conscience is "dread of society [soziale Angst]".7 "Contagion is the second reason,

On the basis of this final assertion, we will subsequently formulate a significant hypothesis.

A third factor — by far the most significant — determines in group members unique traits that can run completely counter to those displayed by an isolated person. I also make reference to that suggestibility, of which the above-mentioned contagion is only an outcome. It is important to keep in mind a few recent physiological discoveries in order to comprehend this phenomena. We now know that a person may be made unconscious by a variety of means, to the point where, once completely devoid of consciousness, he follows the operator's instructions and behaves in ways completely at odds with his habits and character.

This also roughly describes the situation of the person who belongs to a psychological group. He is no longer aware of what he is doing. Similar to the hypnotized person, in his situation, certain faculties may be severely diminished while others may be greatly elevated. He will behave irresistibly impetuously while under the impact of a proposal, carrying out certain tasks. Due to the fact that the suggestion is the same for every member of the group, it becomes stronger through reciprocity, making it more compelling in the case of groups than in that of the hypnotized person.

I have included a lengthy excerpt from this text to emphasize that Le Bon describes the state of an individual in a group as hypnotic, not just drawing a parallel between the two states.

We only want to draw attention to the fact that the two last factors that lead to an individual changing in a group — contagion and increased suggestibility — are obviously not equal because the contagion appears to be a manifestation of suggestibility. We do not intend to raise any objections at this point. Furthermore, it doesn't seem as though Le Bon's comments clearly distinguish between the two components' impacts.

Now that Le Bon has described the group mind, let's move on from the individual. It displays not a single characteristic that a psychoanalyst would have any trouble identifying or tracing back to its origin.

Le Bon himself demonstrates the path by drawing compar-

II. LE BON'S DESCRIPTION OF THE GROUP MIND

isons between it and the mentalities of toddlers and apes (p. 40).

A group is erratic, impetuous, and easily agitated. It is mostly guided by unconscious forces.9. The impulses which a group obeys may according to circumstances be kind or cruel, heroic or cowardly, but they are always so forceful that no particular interest, not even that of selfpreservation, can make itself known (p. 41). It's not planned in the slightest.

A group lacks critical thinking skills, is incredibly gullible and susceptible to persuasion, and it believes things that are implausible. It thinks in pictures that associate with one another (just as they do with people in states of unrestricted imagination) and whose consistency with reality is never verified by any logical function [Instanz].11 A group's emotions are invariably quite basic and exaggerated. in order for a group to be free from both ambiguity and doubt.

12 It goes straight to the extremes; a hint of hostility is transformed into ferocious hatred; a suspicion conveyed is immediately transformed into an unquestionable conviction (p. 56). Thirteen A group, prone as it is to extremes, can only be aroused by an excessive.

To accurately assess the morality of groups, one must recognize that when people join together, all of their personal inhibitions vanish and all of their destructive, vicious, and cruel instincts — which have lain dormant in them like remnants of a bygone era — are awakened in search of unbridled fulfillment. However, suggestion-influenced organizations may also achieve great things in the form of selflessness, sacrifice, and commitment to a cause. When it comes to solitary people, personal interest is typically the single driving factor, but in groups, it is rarely the main one. It's feasible to discuss how a group might elevate a person's moral standards (p. 65).

Lastly, organizations have never been insatiably curious in the truth. They are dependent on illusions and want them. They are almost as affected by falsehoods as they are by truths, and they consistently give the imaginary precedence over the actual. They clearly tend to blur the lines between the two (p. 77).

We have shown that the dominant feature in the psychology of neuroses is the prevalence of the life of phantasy and of the delusion resulting from an unmet want. We have discovered that neurotics are directed by psychological reality rather than regular objective reality. Instead of repeating actual experiences, a hysterical symptom is based on phantasy, and the sensation of guilt in an obsessional manner.

Le Bon's discussion on group leaders is not as thorough and does not help us identify a fundamental idea as clearly. He believes that all living things, whether they are a herd of animals or a group of people, automatically submit to the leadership of a chief when they are assembled in a particular quantity (p. 134). A collective is like a submissive herd that could never survive without its leader. Its need for obedience is so great that it willfully submits to any individual who claims to be its master.

Furthermore, he attributes an enigmatic and compelling force — which he refers to as "prestige" — to the leaders as well as the ideas. Prestige is a form of control that someone, something, or a concept has over us. Our ability to think critically is completely paralyzed, and we are left feeling amazed and respectful. It appears to evoke an emotion akin to hypnotic attraction (p. 148).

He makes a distinction between personal prestige and acquired or manufactured status. Due to custom, the former is linked to people by virtue of their names, wealth, and prestige as

II. LE BON'S DESCRIPTION OF THE GROUP MIND

well as to ideas, artistic creations, etc. As it always refers back to the past, it is not going to help us grasp this perplexing impact very well.

III.

3

Other Accounts of Collective Mental Life

Because Le Bon's explanation aligns so well with our own psychology in emphasizing unconscious mental life, we have used it as an introduction. However, we now have to add that, in actuality, nothing that the author says adds anything new. His attacks on the symptoms of the collective mind are nothing new; intellectuals, politicians, and writers from the dawn of literature have all made similar attacks on the same manifestations of the group mind with equal venom and distinctness before him.17 The two ideas that make up Le Bon's most significant beliefs are those that address how affectivity is being elevated and how intellectual performance is being inhibited collectively.

Furthermore, there has not been a single argument made against Le Bon and the others' assessment of the collective mind or their depiction. Without a doubt, all of the previously mentioned phenomena of the group mind have been accurately observed. However, it is also possible to identify other group formation manifestations that function in an entirely different way and entail a much higher opinion of the group mind.

Le Bon was willing to acknowledge that under some conditions, a group's morality may surpass that of its individual members and that only collectivities had the capacity for extreme selflessness.

Considering these utterly incoherent statements, it appears that group psychology's efforts will ultimately prove futile.

However, it is simple to discover a more optimistic way out of the predicament. It may be necessary to distinguish between a number of quite diverse forms that have likely been combined under the word "group." The claims made by Sighele, Le Bon, and the others concern transient groupings that some casual observers rapidly assembled from a variety of different types of people. Their descriptions have clearly been influenced by the traits of revolutionary groups, particularly those of the great French Revolution. The origins of the opposing viewpoints may be traced to the stable groups or affiliations that people spend their life in.

In his book The Group Mind, McDougall (19) begins with the same conflict that was just discussed and concludes that the aspect of organization provides a solution. According to him, the 'group' may have an organization that is hardly worthy of the name, or it may not have any organization at all. He refers to this sort of assembly as a "crowd." However, he acknowledges that a group of people cannot really join together without at least having some basic organizational skills, and that many of the core concepts of collective psychology may be very easily observed in these uncomplicated groupings (p. 22).

The 'exaltation or amplification of feeling' that each member of the group experiences is the most notable and significant outcome of its development (p. 24). Men's emotions are raised in a group, according to McDougall, to a level that they rarely or never reach in other settings. For those who are involved, giving in to their passions to such an extent and becoming assimilated into the group while losing awareness of their own boundaries is a delightful experience. McDougall describes this as the "principle of direct induction of emotion by way of the primitive," which explains how people are swept away by a shared impulse.

Certain additional group-derived effects also favor this process of emotion amplification. A gang gives someone the impression that they are invincible and have unstoppable power. It temporarily takes the place of human civilization as a whole, which is characterized by the exercise of power, the fear of punishment, and the willingness to submit to numerous inhibitions on the part of the individual. It is obviously dangerous for him to oppose it; instead, it will be safer if he 'hunts with the pack,' as in the case of others around him. He may submit to the new authority and push his previous "conscience" out of his mind, giving in to the allure of the greater pleasure that is unquestionably.

McDougall's summary of the psychological conduct of a basic "unorganised" group is no more compassionate than Le Bon's. Such a group 'is excessively emotional, impulsive, violent, fickle, inconsistent, irresolute, and extreme in action, displaying only the coarser emotions and the less refined sentiments; extremely suggestible, careless in deliberation, hasty in judgment, incapable of any but the simplest and imperfect forms of reasoning; easily swayed and led, lacking in self-consciousness, devoid of self-respect and of sense of responsibility, and apt to be carried away by the consciousness of its own force, so that it tends to produce all the manifestations we have come to expect of any irresponsible and absolute power. As a result, it behaves like a mischievous.

The first and most important need is that the group's existence should be somewhat continuous. This might be material or formal; the former would occur if the same people stay in the organization for an extended period of time, and the latter would occur if the group develops a system of set roles that are held by a series of people.

The second prerequisite is that each group member must have a clear understanding of the nature, makeup, roles, and abilities of the group in order for him to build an emotional bond with the group as a whole.

It appears to us that the state which McDougall describes as the 'organisation' of a group might with greater reason be characterized in another way. The challenge is in acquiring for the group the same attributes that each member brought to the group but which the group formation stifled in him. Because the individual, away from the primitive group, maintained his own continuity, self-awareness, traditions and customs, unique roles and positions, and avoided his competitors. His admission into a "unorganised" group caused him to temporarily lose this uniqueness. Upon acknowledging that the objective is to endow the collective with the characteristics of the individual, we will be reminded.

4

IV. Suggestion and Libido

We began with the basic idea that every member of a group is influenced by it and frequently experiences a significant shift in their mental state. This process clearly leads to an approximation to the other members of the group. The only

IV. SUGGESTION AND LIBIDO

way to achieve this is to remove the inhibitions on his instincts, which are unique to each person, and to give up those expressions of his inclinations that are particularly his own. His emotions become incredibly intense, while his intellectual capacity sharply declines. We've heard that a higher level of group "organization" at least partially prevents these frequently undesirable outcomes, but this doesn't change the core idea of group.

It is evident that the observed events cannot be explained by logical reasons (such the previously described intimidation of the individual, which is the activity of his instinct for self-preservation). Beyond this, the answer that experts in sociology and group psychology usually provide is the same — despite going by different names — and it is the all-important term "suggestion." Tarde refers to it as "imitation," yet we have to concede to a writer who argues that imitation is a byproduct of suggestion and falls under its purview.21 Le Bon attributes all the perplexing aspects of social phenomena to two things: the status of leaders and the mutual suggestion of people. However, once more, prestige is only.

Thus, we will be ready to hear the claim that suggestion — or, more accurately, suggestibility — is, in fact, an irreducible, primal phenomena and a keystone of the human mind. Bernheim also had this view; in 1889, I had the opportunity to observe his amazing talents. However, I still recall being rather hostile to this dictatorship of suggestion even back then. When a patient who revealed himself unamenable was confronted with the shout: 'What are you doing? You yourself contrasuggest!' I told myself, seeing that this was blatantly unfair and violent. For the guy clearly had a right to counter-ideas if they were trying to dominate him with suggestions. Eventually, I started to oppose by demonstrating against.

Christus trug die ganze Welt, Christum trug Christum, so where ist Christus hin hingestellt?23

Christus sustulit orbem, sed Christophorus Christum:

Is it true that ubi Christophorus pedibus dic?

After avoiding the enigma of suggestion for almost thirty years, I've returned to it and discovered that nothing has changed. There is just one exception that I can find to this statement, and as it demonstrates the impact of psycho-analysis, I won't disclose it. I see that special attempts are being made to properly articulate the idea of suggestion, or to rectify the name's traditional use.24 And this is by no means unnecessary, since the term is becoming more and more widely used and has a looser and looser definition. It will eventually be used to refer to any kind of influence at all, much as in English, where the words "to suggest" and "suggestion".

The term "libido" originates from the philosophy of emotions. We refer to this as the energy of those impulses that deal with everything that may be included under the umbrella term "love," which is thought to have a quantitative magnitude but is now unmeasurable. The core of our understanding of love is inherently sexual love with the goal of sexual union. This is what is popularly referred to as love and what poets sing of. However, we are not apart from this — whatever is included in the term "love" — which includes devotion to tangible things and to one's parents, children, friends, and mankind as a whole. On the one hand, we also love ourselves.

Therefore, we believe that language has created the term "love" with all of its many applications in a completely justified piece of unification, and we cannot do better than to utilize it as the foundation for our scientific expositions and arguments.

IV. SUGGESTION AND LIBIDO

Psychoanalysis has unleashed a torrent of wrath by reaching this conclusion, as if it had committed a heinous act of creativity. However, psychoanalysis has not introduced any novel perspectives on love in this "wider" meaning. As Nachmansohn and Pfister have demonstrated in great detail, the 'Eros' of the philosopher Plato corresponds completely with the love force, the libido, of psycho-analysis in terms of its origin, function, and relationship to sexual love;25 and when the apostle Paul,

Because of their origins, psychoanalysis renames these love impulses as sexual instincts, a potiori. Most 'learned' individuals have exacted their retribution by using the tactic of 'pansexualism' to refute psycho-analysis. 'Eros' and 'erotic' are more refined terms that may be used by anyone who views sex as something horrifying and dehumanizing to human nature. I could have avoided a lot of criticism if I had done it myself right away. However, I didn't want to since I want to avoid making allowances for weakness. One never knows where that path will take them; they give in verbally at first, and then gradually in terms of substance as well. I don't think it makes sense to be humiliated.

So, let's try our luck on the assumption that the core of the collective mind also consists of romantic relationships — or, to put it more neutrally, emotional bonds. Recall that no such relationships are mentioned by the authorities. It is obvious that what would make sense to them is hidden behind the suggestion-screen, or shelter.

In the first case, two stray thoughts provide credence to our idea. First, it is evident that a force of some type is holding the group together. What force could be more fittingly attributed to this achievement than Eros, who is the source of all worldly unity? Second, that if a person in a group surrenders his individuality and allows the other members to persuade him, it.

5

V. Two Artificial Groups: The Church and the Army

It may be recalled from our understanding of the morphology of groups that distinct group types and opposing lines may be identified at different stages of their evolution. There exist groups that are extremely short-lived and long-lasting, homogeneous — composed of people of the same type — and heterogeneous — natural and artificial — that depend on an outside force to maintain their unity. There are also groups that are highly organized and have a clear structure. However, for still-to-be-explained reasons, we would especially like to emphasize a distinction that the authorities have, for the most part, paid much too little attention to: that between groups without leaders and those that do. Furthermore, in total contrast to custom, we will not.

Both the army and the church are artificial organizations; as such, they depend on an outside power to keep them together and to prevent structural changes. A person is typically not given the option to leave such a group or is not allowed a say in the matter; any effort to do so is typically treated with persecution, harsh punishment, or very specific restrictions. We are not now interested in finding out why these connections require such specific protections. We are simply drawn to one situation, which is that some truths, which are far more hidden in other situations, are readily apparent in those highly organized groupings that are shielded from disintegration.

Upon closer inspection, it becomes evident that every member of these two manufactured organizations is connected to both the commander-in-chief, Christ, and the other group members by libidinal[29] bonds. It is necessary to save these questions for further research: how these two relationships connect to one another, if they are the same sort and worth, and how they should be psychologically represented.

However, we will even now take a modest stance and criticize the authorities for failing to recognize the leader's significance

V. TWO ARTIFICIAL GROUPS: THE CHURCH AND THE ARMY

in the group's psychology, even if our own selection of the initial subject for study has placed us in a better position.

Panic, a phenomena most studied in military units, provides a clue to the same effect — that a group's essence is located in the libidinal relationships that exist inside it. If a group of that sort splits apart, fear ensues. Its traits include everyone being solicitous just for their personal benefit and disregarding the opinions of others, and none of the commands issued by superiors being followed.

A massive and thoughtless fear [Angst] is released as the mutual bonds have vanished. Naturally, the complaint that it is actually the other way around and that the level of fear has increased will be raised at this point once more.

These statements do not at all refute the claim that induction (contagion) causes fear in a community to grow to huge dimensions. When there is a significant risk and no strong emotional bonds among the group — conditions that are met, for example, when a fire breaks out at a theater or other entertainment center — McDougall's point of view is fully supported. The instance that is most useful to us is the one that was previously stated, in which a group of soldiers panics despite the fact that the level of danger has not escalated beyond what is customary and frequently seen.

Individuals who, like McDougall (l.c.), characterize panic as one of the most basic operations of the "group mind" reach the contradictory conclusion that this group mind eliminates itself in one of its most glaring forms. It is undeniable that panic entails the breakdown of a group; it entails the abolition of any regard that the group's members would normally exhibit for one another.

The normal occurrence of a panic attack is quite similar to

how it is portrayed in Nestroy's parody of Hebbel's Judith and Holofernes play. "The general has lost his head!" exclaims a soldier, and all of the Assyrians immediately flee. The demise of the leader in any capacity,

The event that follows the breakdown of a religious organization that is intended to occur here is not fear, for which there is no need to be afraid. Instead, they exhibit vicious and antagonistic tendencies toward other people, something they had previously been unable to do because of Christ's equal love.33 Nevertheless, even in Christ's kingdom, those who do not love him, do not belong to the believing community, and whom he does not love, remain outside of this bond. Thus, even if a religion claims to be the religion of love, it must yet be harsh and unloving toward non-members. In essence, all religions are love-based and embrace all people equally.

6

VI. Further Problems and Lines of Work

Up till now, we have focused on two artificial groupings and discovered that two emotional ties dominate them. In these circumstances, at least, one of these factors — the tie with the leader — seems to have more of an impact on decisions than the other, which is held amongst group members.

There is still plenty to look at and explain in the morphology of groupings. As long as these connections have not been made, we should have to start with the known truth that a simple group of individuals is not a group; but, we also have to acknowledge that the inclination for any group of people to become a psychological group can very quickly take center stage.

However, none of these concerns — which may also have been partially addressed in group psychology literature — will be able to deflect our attention from the underlying psychological issues that arise from the makeup of a group. And the first thing that will grab our attention is a thought that should lead us straight to evidence supporting the claim that libidinal relationships are what define a group.

Let's bear in mind the character of the emotional bonds that exist between males in general. In Schopenhauer's well-known parable of the icy porcupines, nobody can stand it when their neighbor gets too close.

Psycho-analysis provides evidence that nearly all intimate emotional relationships that endure over time, such as marriage, friendships, and parent-child relationships, leave a residue of feelings of repulsion and dislike that must first be suppressed. This is less covered up by regular arguments between business associates or by complaints from a subordinate to a supervisor. When guys form larger groups, the same thing occurs.

Each family believes it was born better or is superior to the other whenever two families are united by marriage. Each of the two adjacent cities is the most envious adversary of the other; each little canton holds the others in low regard. Racial relatives have a close relationship.

When this animosity is aimed against those who are otherwise loved, we label it as ambivalence of emotion and, in a possibly overly logical way, we explain it away by pointing out how many times conflicts of interest develop precisely in these kinds of close relationships. Unmistakable antipathies and aversions that people have toward strangers with whom they must interact might be seen as narcissistic expressions of self-love. This self-love promotes the person's self-assertion and acts as though any departure from his own specific developmental paths is criticism of them and a request that they be changed. We're not sure why these particular situations should have been the focus of such sensitivity.

However, as a group forms and grows, all of this intolerance disappears, either permanently or momentarily. People act as though they are uniform, accept the quirks of others, place themselves on an equal footing with them, and don't feel any animosity against them as long as a group formation stands or grows. In our theoretical framework, a libidinal relationship with other individuals is the sole thing that may cause such a restriction of narcissism. Love for things and love for people are the only barriers that love for oneself understands.37 It will immediately be questioned whether a community of interest by itself, without any libido added, must not inevitably result in the tolerance of other.

However, our curiosity now prompts us to consider the urgent topic of what the nature of these links inside groups may be. Previously, the focus of psychoanalytic research on neuroses has mostly been on the connections between the objects of love and their underlying sexual desires. Clearly, there can be no discussion of such sexual goals in organizations. Though they still function with the same vigor, the love impulses we are discussing here have strayed from their intended course. We have now seen events that fall outside of the typical sexual object-cathexis [Objektbesetzung] and indicate a deviation of the instinct from its sexual goal.

7

VII. Identification

Psychoanalysis recognizes identification as the initial manifestation of an emotional bond with another individual. It has an impact on the Oedipus complex's early development. A young kid will show a particular interest in his father; he wants to emulate him and become just like him in every way.

All we have to say is that he looks up to his father. This behavior is distinctly masculine and has nothing to do with being submissive or feminine toward his father or guys in general. It helps pave the way for the Oedipus complex, which it fits in with quite nicely.

It's easy to forget about the history that followed this identification with the father. In the event that the Oedipus complex is reversed and the father is perceived as the source of a feminine attitude and the object that satisfies one's direct sexual urges, identification with the father has become the precursor to an object tie with the father. With the appropriate modifications, the same applies to the infant daughter as well.

The difference between choosing the father as an object and identifying with him is simple to express in a formula. One's father is what they aspire to be in the first scenario, while in the second, he is.

Let's separate identification as it manifests itself in a neurotic symptom's structure from its convoluted relationships. Assuming that a little child (whom we shall remain anonymous for the time being) experiences the same excruciating symptom as her mother—for example, the same excruciating cough.

This might occur in a number of ways. The identification could be a result of the Oedipus complex; in that case, it would indicate a hostile desire on the girl's part to replace her mother. The symptom also expresses her object love towards her father and helps her realize, under the weight of guilt, how much she wants to replace her mother: "As far as the pain goes, you wanted to be your mother, and now you are."

A third, very common, and significant instance of symptom development occurs when the identification completely ignores any item relationship to the person being duplicated. Assuming,

VII. IDENTIFICATION

for example, that a girl at a boarding school receives a letter from a person she secretly loves, which causes her to become enraged and cause her to go into a hysteric fit, some of her friends who are aware of it will, as we say, "contract the fit" by mental infection. The identification process is predicated on the ability or desire to place oneself in the same circumstance.

We may guess that this shared emotional aspect stems from the nature of the relationship with the leader. We already start to sense that the mutual tie amongst members of a group is in the form of an identification of this sort. Another theory might suggest that we haven't solved the identification puzzle entirely and that we still need to deal with the psychological process known as "empathy" (Einfühlung), which is mostly responsible for our comprehension of what makes other people fundamentally different from ourselves. However, we will focus just on the immediate emotional consequences of identification here, ignoring its importance for our intellectual lives.

In a significant number of cases, the origins of male homosexuality are as follows. In the concept of an Oedipus complex, a young man has been abnormally long-term and strongly focused with his mother. But when his adolescence ends, it's finally time to trade his mother in for a different sexual object. The young man's actions take an unexpected turn: instead of leaving his mother, he turns into her and identifies with her. He then searches for things that may take the place of his ego and provide it the same kind of love and attention that he has received from his mother. This is a regular procedure that may be verified as frequently as desired, and it is.

However, these melancholys also reveal something else to us, which can be relevant to our next conversations. They portray the ego as split into two fragments, with one of them fighting the other. The second component is the one that possesses the missing thing and has been transformed by introjection. But we are also familiar with the item that acts in such a horrible manner.

It consists of the conscience, a critical faculty [Instanz] 43 inside the ego that, even in ordinary circumstances, adopts a critical stance against the ego, but seldom with such tenacity or justification. We have previously been led to the hypothesis44 that our ego develops a talent of its own that allows it to isolate itself from the rest.

8

VIII. Being in Love and Hypnosis

The use of language is accurate to some degree of reality despite its whims. As a result, it labels a wide variety of emotional interactions that we can all theoretically lump together as loving relationships under the term "love." However, it also raises questions about whether these relationships are sincere and genuine, hinting at a wide range of possibilities within the phenomenon of love.

It will be easy for us to make the same finding by empirical means.

One kind of situations involves falling in love as little more than an object-cathexis by the sexual impulses to get immediate sexual gratification; this cathexis also ends as the goal is accomplished; this is referred to as common,

In addition to this, there is another element that comes from the incredible path of evolution that the sensual life of man pursues. A youngster finds the first object of his love in one or both of his parents during his first phase, which generally ends by the time he is five years old. All of his sexual impulses and their need for gratification have been unified onto this object. His relationship with his parents is profoundly altered as a result of the suppression that eventually sets in, forcing him to give up the majority of his childish sexual desires.

As we all know, new, powerful inclinations with overtly sexual goals emerge throughout puberty. In unfavorable circumstances, they continue to exist independently of the enduring "tender" emotional tendencies as a sensual stream.

The image that follows is one that some literary groups take great pleasure in idealizing due to its two characteristics. A guy of this sort will display a sentimental fervor for women whom he highly respects but who do not stimulate him to sexual activities, and he will only be potent with other women that he does not 'love' but thinks poorly of or even despises.48 But more frequently than not, the teenager manages to create a certain level of harmony between the physical, celestial love.

Idealization is the inclination that distorts judgment in this way. However, this facilitates our navigation throughout the area. We see that the object receives the same treatment as our own ego, which causes a significant amount of our narcissistic desire to spill over onto the object when we fall in love. In many cases of love choosing, it is even evident that the object stands in for some unfulfilled ego ideal on our part. We adore it because it satisfies our narcissism by providing the perfections we have long aspired to for our own ego and would now want to get in this devious manner.

This is particularly common in cases of unsatisfied and sad love as every sexual fulfillment always results in a decrease in sexual exaggeration. The functions assigned to the ego ideal completely stop working in tandem with this "devotion" of the ego to the object, which can no longer be separated from a sublimated devotion to an abstract notion. That faculty does not voice criticism; all that the object requests and does is good and innocent.

Anything done for the purpose of the object is exempt from conscience; in the blindness of love, remorselessness reaches the height of criminality. A formula may be used to summarize the entire situation:

It is even feasible to characterize an extreme form of love as a situation in which the ego has introjected the object into itself. Economically, there is no issue of poverty or enrichment. Perhaps a different difference better captures the substance of the issue. In identification, the item has been lost or abandoned; it is then reassembled inside the ego, which modifies itself somewhat in response to the lost thing's model. In the other scenario, the item is kept but is hyper-cathexized by the ego at its expense. However, a problem arises here as well. Is it a given that object-cathexis is necessary for identification?

It seems like it's just a small step from being in love to hypnosis. It's clear that the two agree on several regards. The same deference, obedience, and lack of judgment are shown to the hypnotist as they are to the object of their affection. One's own initiative is similarly absorbed; it is undeniable that the hypnotist has taken the place of the ego ideal. The explanation of being in love through hypnosis is more direct since everything is even clearer and more vivid during this state, rather than the reverse. The only subject receiving attention is the hypnotist, and he is the only one.

However, if the phrase is acceptable, we may also state that the hypnotic connection is a two-person group formation.

Since it is more accurate to claim that hypnosis is the same as group formation, it is not an appropriate object to compare it to. It singles just one aspect of the complex group fabric for us to focus on: each member's behavior toward the leader. This restriction on the number separates hypnosis from group formation, just as the absence of overtly sexual impulses separates it from love. It falls somewhere in the middle of the two in this regard.

If hypnosis didn't show certain characteristics that the logical explanation of it as a state of being in love with the explicitly sexual inclinations omitted doesn't fit, we wouldn't be able to solve the puzzle of the libidinal structure of groups right quickly. We still have to acknowledge that a lot of it is mysterious and unexplainable.

It has an extra layer of paralysis that comes from the relationship between a powerful person and someone weak and defenseless, which might lead to a shift into the terrifying hypnosis that happens to animals. The process by which it is generated, its connection to sleep, and the perplexing method in which;

VIII. BEING IN LOVE AND HYPNOSIS

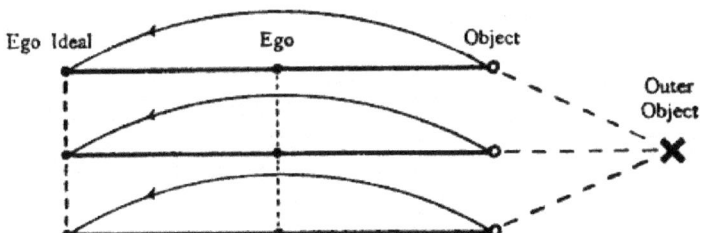

9

IX. The Herd Instinct

IX. THE HERD INSTINCT

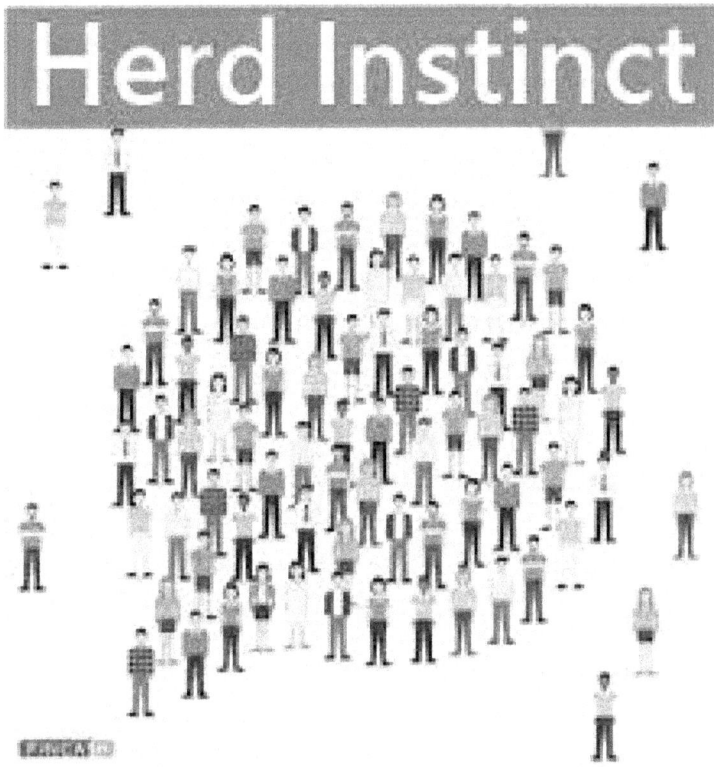

We are unable to maintain the delusion for very long that we have used this formula to answer the group's mystery. The sudden and unsettling realization that all we have actually accomplished is to refocus attention on the enigma surrounding hypnosis, which still has a lot of unanswered questions, is unavoidable. And now, yet another argument points out where we need to go.

One could argue that the strong emotional bonds that form within groups adequately account for some of their traits, such as the members' lack of initiative and independence, the similarities in their responses, and their "reduction" to the level of group members. However, if we view it as;

As a result, we get the idea that people are in a situation where their unique emotions and intellectual acts are too weak to do anything on their own and must wait to be reinforced by other group members acting in a similar manner.

We are reminded of how commonplace these dependent phenomena are in human society, how little creativity and individual bravery it contains, and how much each person is influenced by the attitudes of the collective mind that take the shape of racial traits, class prejudices, public opinion, and so on. When we acknowledge the effect of suggestion, it becomes even more of a mystery to us.

According to Trotter, the mental processes that are characterized as happening in groups are caused by the "gregariousness" or herd instinct, which is intrinsic in both humans and other animal species. This gregariousness is a biological continuation of multicellularity, and may be compared to it. According to the libido hypothesis, it is an additional expression of the tendency for all living things of the same sort to unite into ever-larger groups. This tendency stems from the libido.51 A person who is alone feels "incomplete." It would appear that tiny children's fear is already an indication of this herd drive.

Since resisting the herd is just as beneficial as breaking away from it, it is.

Though we tend to agree with the contrary conclusion — that it is hard to understand the nature of a group if the leader is ignored — Trotter's presentation, which is even more reasonable than the others, is vulnerable to criticism that it ignores the leader's role in the group. The leader has no place at all in the herd instinct; he is just thrown in with the herd, almost by accident. It therefore follows that there is no way to go from

IX. THE HERD INSTINCT

this instinct to the requirement for a god, as the herd does not have a herdsman. However, aside from this, Trotter's argument may be psychologically refuted, making it likely that the herd instinct is not unchangeable.

The emergence of concepts such as esprit de corps, "group spirit," Gemeingeist, and so on later in society does not negate the fact that these concepts sprang from jealousy. Nobody should feel the need to stand out; everyone should want to be the same. In order to achieve social justice, we must deprive ourselves a great deal in order to prevent others from having to endure the same hardships or, conversely, from having the ability to request things. The foundation of social conscience and a sense of obligation is this desire for equality. It shows itself unexpectedly in the fear of spreading the disease to others that syphilitic persons experience, which psychoanalysis has helped us to comprehend. These despicable wretches' fear is matched by their ferocious fights.

Therefore, the foundation of social emotion is the conversion of an initially antagonistic sensation into a pleasantly toned bond of identification. This reversal looks to be the result of a common tender bond with someone outside the group, as far as we have been able to trace the course of events. Although we do not consider our identification analysis to be comprehensive, for the sake of this discussion, we should return to this one aspect of identification — namely, its need that equalization be carried out consistently. As we've previously learned in the conversation about the two artificial groups — the army and the church — the prerequisite for membership is that each member must get the same level of affection.

X. The Group and the Primal Horde

> **GROUP FORMATION**
>
> Group formation is a revival of the primal horde, in which primal father is the group ideal which governs the ego in place of the ego ideal.

X. THE GROUP AND THE PRIMAL HORDE

I adopted Darwin's theory in 1912 that the first form of human civilization was a horde under the tyrannical leadership of a dominant male. I tried to demonstrate how the fortunes of this horde have left irreversible marks on the history of human descent; specifically, that the violent killing of the chief and the transformation of the paternal horde into a brotherhood are linked to the development of totemism, which includes the origins of morality, religion, and social organization.53 As with many other theories used by archaeologists to try and shed light on the shadow of prehistoric periods, this one is, of course, only a hypothesis — a "Just-So Story," as one amusingly described it.

For this reason, the gathering seems to us like a return of the primordial horde. The primal horde may reappear out of any random throng, just as primitive man essentially exists in every person. To the extent that men are accustomed to being governed by group formation, we acknowledge the existence of the primeval horde in this way. We have to come to the conclusion that group psychology is the oldest branch of human psychology. Individual psychology, which we have isolated and ignored by ignoring all evidence of the group, emerged gradually and is still, at best, partially explained from the old group psychology. Later on, we'll try to pinpoint the exact starting point.

He was the Superman that Nietzsche could only have imagined for the far future, at the dawn of human history. Even in this day and age, followers still require the delusion that their leader loves them equally and justly; nevertheless, the leader does not require love from anybody else; he or she may be a masterful, utterly narcissistic, self-assured, and independent person.

We already know that love restrains narcissism, so it would be easy to demonstrate how love contributed to civilization in this way.

Until he was deified, the horde's primordial parent was not yet immortal. In the event that he passed away, someone had to take his position, most likely the youngest.

The prospect of sexual fulfillment was also extended to whoever succeeded him, providing a method of escaping the confines of group psychology. The fact that his libido was fixed on women and that he could satisfy it without waiting or building up made it unnecessary for him to pursue his suppressed sexual urges, which in turn allowed his narcissism to always reach its peak. We will address this relationship between character development and love in a postscript.

We should also draw attention to the particularly instructive relationship that exists between the structure of the primordial horde and the device used to keep an artificial group together.

However, we anticipate much more of this group's ancestry from the primordial horde. It should also assist us in comprehending what remains perplexing and inexplicable about group formations — all that is concealed under the cryptic terms suggestion and hypnosis. It can also succeed in this, in my opinion. Remember that there is something pleasantly eerie about hypnosis; nonetheless, the uncanny quality alludes to a long-standing, familiar aspect that has been suppressed.56 Let's examine the induction of hypnosis.

The hypnotist claims to have an enigmatic ability that allows him to deprive the subject of their free will, or, conversely, the subject comes to think this about him. This enigmatic ability, which is still frequently discussed in the public.

It is true that there are alternative methods to induce hypnosis, such as staring at a bright object or listening to a repetitive sound.

X. THE GROUP AND THE PRIMAL HORDE

This is deceptive and has led to the development of insufficient physiological hypotheses. Actually, the only purpose of these processes is to capture and maintain conscious attention. It's as though the hypnotist had told the victim, "Now worry yourself only with my person; the rest of the world is quite uninteresting." Technically speaking, a hypnotist could never give a speech like that since it would take the patient away from his unconscious attitude and encourage conscious opposition. The hypnotist refrains from controlling the person's awareness.

The real revelation made by Ferenczi is that the hypnotist is assuming the role of the subject's parents when he commands the subject to go to sleep, a common practice during the onset of hypnosis. He believes that there are two different types of hypnosis to be identified: a calming and persuading kind that is modeled after the mother, and a menacing type that is modeled after the father.

59 The directive to go to sleep when in a hypnotic state now essentially means to turn off all external attention and focus it only on the hypnotist. And the subject understands it this way because sleep is a psychological phenomenon that is associated with this disengagement from the outside world.

GROUP PHYCHOLOGY AND THE ANALYSIS OF THE EGO

XI.

11

A Differentiating Grade in the Ego

If we examine a modern man's life while keeping in mind the authorities' mutually supportive explanations of group psychology, we could become too afraid to try a thorough explication due to the intricacies that become apparent. Every individual has built up their ego ideal based on a variety of models, is a part of several organizations, and is connected to multiple identities. As a result, every person has a place in many group thoughts, including those of his race, class, creed, nationality, etc., but he may also elevate himself above them to the point where he retains some degree of uniqueness and independence.

We understand that the explanation of the libidinal structure of groups that we have been able to provide goes back to the difference between the ego and the ego ideal, as well as the two types of ties that this allows for: identification and the replacement of the ego ideal with the object. As a first step in a study of the ego, the assumption of this form of discriminating grade [Stufe] in the ego must progressively show its validity in the most diverse areas of psychology. In my work "Zur Einführung des Narzissmus," I have compiled all of the pathological evidence that is currently available to support this division.

I'll simply address one of the implications that appear plausible from this angle here, continuing the conversation about an issue that I had to leave unresolved in another location.61 Every mental difference that we are familiar with is a new development that exacerbates the problems with mental functioning, makes it more unstable, and may serve as the catalyst for mental breakdown, or the commencement of a disease. Therefore, the act of birth marks the transition from a fully self-sufficient narcissism to the awareness of a changing outside environment and the start of object discovery. It is entirely possible that the ego ideal and ego must be momentarily separated since neither of them can be sustained for very long. A periodic violation of the prohibition is the norm in all renunciations and limitations placed upon the ego; this is demonstrated by the establishment of festivals, which are, at their core, nothing more nor less than legal excesses, and which derive their joyous nature from the relief they afford.62 This fundamental similarity exists between the Roman Saturnalia and our contemporary carnival and the festivals of the primitive people, which frequently result in various forms of revelry and the breaking of what are sometimes the most holy laws.

Therefore, we don't know the basis for these naturally occurring mood swings, nor do we understand the process by which mania replaces melancholy. We are therefore free to assume that these patients are individuals for whom our hypothesis may have real significance — that is, that their ego ideal may have momentarily resolved into their ego after previously ruling it with particular rigor.

Let's stick to what is obvious: Based on our ego analysis, it is undeniable that during manic episodes, the ego and the ego ideal have combined, allowing the person to experience the removal of all inhibitions and feelings of concern for others while in a state of triumph and self-satisfaction and free from self-criticism.

A shift into mania is not a necessary component of melancholy depression's symptomatology. Simple melancholias never exhibit this progression; some occur in a single episode, while others occur in recurrent bouts. However, there are melancholias when the exhilarating cause is obviously a contributing factor. They are the ones that happen when a loved one passes away or experiences other situations that force the libido to be withheld from the object. Such psychogenic melancholia can lead to mania, and this cycle can recur several times, just as readily as in a seemingly spontaneous episode. As a result, the situation is somewhat unclear, especially since there are so few types.

However, I do not see any problem in attributing a portion of both psychogenic and spontaneous melancholia to the aspect of the ego's occasional rebellion against the ego ideal. It is possible to speculate that in the spontaneous form, the ego ideal has a tendency to exhibit an odd strictness, which inevitably leads to its temporary suspension. In the psychogenic variety, the ego would be provoked to rebel against its ideal when it experiences mistreatment from its association with a rejected object.

12

XII. Postscript

During the recently concluded provisional investigation, we discovered some unanticipated avenues that we first chose not to pursue. However, there were other opportunities that had potential for providing us with valuable insights. In this way, we would want to address a few of the points that have been left on one side.

A. The two major artificial groupings that we started by examining, the army and the Christian church, provide an intriguing example of the difference between the ego's identification with an object and its replacement by an object.

It is evident that a soldier views his superior — basically, the army commander — as his ideal, but;

How he spuckt and how he räuspert,

You have made him happy with that!

Within the Catholic Church, it is different. Every Christian sees Christ as their ideal and feels an unbreakable bond of connection with all other Christians. However, the Church needs more from him. In addition, he must love all other Christians in the same way that Christ loved them. As a result, the Church mandates that the libido provided by a group formation be strengthened at both points. once object-choice has occurred, identification must also be provided, and once identification is present, object love must be added. It is clear that this amendment goes outside the group's charter. It is possible to be a devout Christian and still reject the notion of placing oneself in Christ's shoes and desiring to be like him.

We need to briefly revisit the scientific myth of the father of the primordial horde in order to achieve this goal. Because he had given birth to every son that made up the first group, he was eventually elevated to the position of creator of the world and with justice. He was revered and feared equally by all of them, and it was this combination of qualities that gave rise to the concept of taboo. Eventually, these several people

XII. POSTSCRIPT

formed a group, murdered him, and dismembered him. All of the winners were unable to succeed him, and if any did, the conflicts would just start over until they realized they had to give up their father's lineage.

It was at that point that someone could have felt compelled to leave the group and assume the role of the father out of a desperate desire. The first epic poet was the one who accomplished this, and his inventiveness was the advancement. This poet's desire led him to cover up the truth with falsehoods. The heroic myth was created by him. The father, who continued to reappear in the tale as a totemic monster, was killed by the hero, a man who had done it all by himself. The poet constructed the first ego ideal in the hero who desires to be the father, just as the father had been the boy's first ideal. The youngest one was probably able to make the shift from villain to hero.

Thus, the myth represents the process by which the individual separates from collective psychology. The hero or psychological story was undoubtedly the original myth; the nature myth that provided an explanation had to have come considerably later. Rank has noted that even after taking this action and releasing himself from the group in his mind, the poet is still able to find his way back to it in the real world. Because he goes and tells the gathering about his created hero's actions. This hero is ultimately just himself.

As a result, he brings his audience up to the level of fantasy while lowering himself to that of reality. However, those who listen to him comprehend the poet, and since they have.

C. This work has discussed explicitly sexual impulses and those that are inhibited in their goals in great detail, and hopefully this distinction will not be met with too much opposition. Even if a thorough examination of the issue would just restate what has essentially already been said, it would still be appropriate.

The libido development of infants has introduced us to the earliest, and finest, example of sexual desires that are suppressed in their goals. Any and all emotions a youngster has for its parents and caregivers easily translate into desires that show the child's inclination toward sexuality.

As is well known, this first arrangement of the child's love, which is often coordinated with the Oedipus complex, gives way to a wave of suppression from the start of the latency phase onward. The remainder manifests as a simply delicate emotional relationship that is no longer 'sexual' yet nevertheless connects to the same persons. Psychoanalysis, which sheds light on the inner workings of the mind, has little trouble demonstrating how the repressed and unconscious sexual bonds from early childhood still exist. It gives us the confidence to say that whatever tenderness we experience is the result of a fully "sensual" object relationship with the person in question, or rather.

Tender emotional bonds, however generated from inclinations that have a sexual objective, are generally the expression of tendencies that have no sexual aim, according to a psychology that will not or cannot enter the depths of what is suppressed.71

It is reasonable to argue that individuals have strayed from their sexual goals, even if it might be challenging to articulate how this deviation from purpose complies with metapsychological standards. Furthermore, impulses that are suppressed in their pursuits always retain part of their initial sexual urges; even a friend or admirer who is deeply in love wants to be physically close to and in the company of the person they are now merely infatuated with.

XII. POSTSCRIPT

Naturally, we won't be shocked to learn that the sexual tendencies that are suppressed in their goals stem from the purely sexual ones when the goals are rendered unachievable by internal or external barriers. An internal barrier of this type, or rather one that has internalized, is the suppression experienced throughout the latency stage. Due to his sexual intolerance, we infer that the father of the primeval horde forced all of his sons to abstain, forcing them into relationships that hindered their goals, while he reserved his own freedom of sexual satisfaction and stayed unconnected. Every link that holds a group together is made up of impulses that are restrained in their goals.

By joining together for the sole aim of gratifying their sexual desires, two individuals are defying the collective tendency and sensation of herd mentality. They are more adequate for one another the more in love they are. Shame serves as a physical manifestation of the rejection of the group's power. To prevent a group bond from encroaching on the preferred sexual object, the intensely violent emotions of jealousy are triggered. It is only conceivable for two individuals to engage in sexual activity in front of other people when the delicate, or intimate, aspect of a love relationship completely gives way to the sensual one.

The church and the army are two large artificial groupings where women are not allowed to be used as sexual objects. Men and women's romantic relationships continue outside of these organizations. Gender differences have little bearing, even in situations when mixed-gender organizations are established. Asking whether the desire that unites groups is heterosexual or gay is hardly relevant since it does not distinguish between the sexes and, in particular, demonstrates a total disdain for the goals of the genital organization of the libido.

Sexual urges allow a person to retain some of their individuality even if they have otherwise integrated themselves into a community.

We have learned from the psycho-analytic study of psycho-neuroses that the symptoms of these disorders might be directly linked to suppressed but still-active sexual urges. By adding to this formula, we may finish it off: alternatively, ct inclinations that have been suppressed in their goals but whose suppression has either not fully succeeded or has allowed the suppressed sexual goal to resurface. Accordingly, a neurosis should cause its victim to become asocial and separate him from typical social groups. One may argue that neurotic has the same destabilizing impact on a community as romantic love. However, it seems that neuroses may lessen in situations when group formation has received a strong boost.

The foundation of being in love is the coexistence of both overtly sexual impulses and suppressed sexual impulses, which allows the object to attract a portion of the narcissistic ego-libido to itself. There is only space for the ego and the object in this situation.

Hypnosis is similar to love in that it is exclusive to these two individuals, but it is only driven by sexual impulses that are restrained and replace the ego ideal with the object.

The group doubles this process; it is consistent with hypnosis in that the object replaces the ego ideal and that instincts keep it together; however, it also incorporates affiliation with other people.

THANK YOU

XII. POSTSCRIPT

THE END

www.ingramcontent.com/pod-product-compliance
Lightning Source LLC
LaVergne TN
LVHW020438080526
838202LV00055B/5257